THEY CAME
TO KILL ME

THEY CAME TO KILL ME

Dorothy A. Weatherford

authorHOUSE®

AuthorHouse™
1663 Liberty Drive
Bloomington, IN 47403
www.authorhouse.com
Phone: 1-800-839-8640

First published by AuthorHouse   02/03/2012

ISBN: 978-1-4685-5066-5 (sc)
ISBN: 978-1-4685-5067-2 (ebk)

Library of Congress Control Number: 2012902176

Printed in the United States of America

CONTENTS

How Do You Pray Against Territorial Spirits

1. Pray protection over each Person, Loved ones, Churches and Intercessors praying on their Behalf.
2. Repent (Repent on Behalf of the City's sin)
3. Local Pastors who have Strong Anointing and Authority to Lead in the Prayer against the Territorial Spirits and Command their Powers to be Broken.
4. Plant GOD'S WORD into the City in two ways:
   A. Fill the vacancy that is made when the wicked spirits depart by planting the WORD of GOD in its place.
   B. Speak Restoration of the City to its Original Calling. If you do not directly address the Principalities and Powers over a City NOTHING will HAPPEN.

DISPLACE—To move from usual Place or Position, to Force to Leave.

DECEIVE—To cause to believe what is not true, Mislead, Lead into Error, Danger or Disadvantageous Position offer by Underhanded Means, Lead in Wrong Direction or into Error of Thoughts or Actions.

GALATIANS 3:1—Who has bewitched you that you should not Obey the TRUTH?

6. Pray against anti-christ Spirits its influence over Countries, Cities and Churches.
7. Must displace the anti-christ spirits.

Sabotage—The destruction of property or obstruction of normal operation as by enemy agents in war, treacherous actions *to defeat or hinder* a cause or an endeavor, deliberate subversion. ANTICHRIST

CHAPTER ONE

THE FIGHT WITH THE WOMAN

———◆◆✕◆◆———

This is where the Warfare began: GOD dealt with me in dreams pertaining to Warfare.

I was a newly installed Ordained Pastor, I had just gotten ordained to the Office of a Pastor: October 22, 1995. In December of 1995, I dreamed we all (congregation) were eating at this restaurant. This woman walked up and started fighting me for no reason. They took me to Jail in the dream, I remember being very frighten! In my mind I said I will go and tell them about JESUS. When they took me to Population I went in and they were sleeping and I began to tell them about JESUS. I kept on Preaching and Teaching and telling them, Then they were awaken as I continued teaching they pulled their covers back and they had Bibles in their beds. I continued to teach then one lady said we have been waiting for someone to come and teach us, as I continued to teach, Babies came from under their beds. I woke up out of the dream yet not knowing what to think of the dream. I knew it had a Spiritual Significance, Little did I know what was going to transpire. The woman in the dream was the Jezebel spirit that came to fight against me. Just like Elijah when he was confronted with this spirit he was afraid. This spirit always promotes Fear and intimidation. The Jezebel spirit always tries to make you think it can take your life (1 Kings 19:2) Which will cause you to take flight (1 Kings 19:3). Because you allow yourself to be intimidated and full of fear you will take flight. Mind you the running is mostly never positive. Elijah wanted and requested that his life might be taken (vs. 4 of 1 Kings 19). When we understand how this spirit operates we can KILL this spirit!

SHE MAKES US THINK:

1. She can take over our Lives
2. Makes us run from GOD or the work of GOD
3. Run to the Wilderness to bring desolation in our Lives in every area
4. Make us want to give up
5. Operate in self pity
6. Make us hide (1 Kings 19:9)
7. Steal our zeal (1 Kings 19:10)

As I refer to the pronoun 'she', I am not talking about gender, this spirit has no gender.

Many identify with this spirit as a woman because of the origin or history of this spirit that manifested itself through a woman named Jezebel. This spirit will try to cut the True Prophets of GOD off; those who are called of GOD and teaching Truth. Let's understand every Preacher or Prophets are not called of GOD! Remember the Prophets of Baal (1 Kings 18:20-40) There are Prophets today who are not the Prophets of GOD but are Standing as though they are Prophets of GOD exercising their gifts in the House of GOD.

We must understand their administration is to stop you from Teaching Truth and Giving Birth to your Destiny. We must realize we have to Anoint, Establish other People for Ministry as seen in (1 Kings 19:15, 16) Elijah had to anoint Hazael to be King over Syria, Jehu to be King over Israel, Elisha to be Prophet in his room and that they may give Birth to their Destiny. Remember the whole Creation is WAITING for the Manifestation of the Sons of GOD (Rom 8:19). The Sons of GOD are not people who just confess Christ, but they Obey Christ and his Lordship, In Philippians 2: 12-15 They would show the Obedience of Christ. Paul does not teach that SALVATION is not dependent upon works, but that Salvation must be through Christian living an upright Character in the Body of CHRIST. We must be blameless and innocent as the Sons of GOD, in the Midst of a Crooked and Perverse Generation among whom we shine as Lights in the World (Phil 2:25). Far too long the Body of Christ has compromised the standards of Holy Living, Perverting the Gospel of Truth and the Ordinances of GOD. We have allowed the Jezebel spirit to run rampant throughout the Local Assemblies because of our state of Apostasy. Mostly all Pastors including myself have allowed the spirit to teach and seduce GOD'S Servant (Rev 2:20). It's a Prophetic Call of Repentance; If we Repent we will be given POWER over NATIONS (Rev 2:26).

Dorothy A. Weatherford

This is a PERFECT TIME to REPENT:

Ask GOD to forgive us for allowing this spirit to intimidate us, put fear in us, make us regress, hide from GOD as Adam and Eve did in the Garden (Gen 3:10). Operating in self pity, lose our zeal. Ask GOD to Restore us that we may have PEACE in our LIVES and AFFAIRS. To defeat this spirit we must not tolerate or allow this spirit to have access and liberty to teach GOD'S people. We must understand when we allow or permit the spirit to impart Knowledge, Instruct or Preach it brings Harm, Injury, and Death to the body. We must take authority over this spirit through Prayer, Fasting and Standing against it. We must not allow the opportunity for her to impart her doctrines (Eph 4:27) we are told to give no place or opportunity to the devil. If we have allowed this spirit access we must bind it up in the Name of JESUS, Plead the BLOOD of JESUS, So that false spirit will no longer have access. Even bind the residue of this spirit so that it will no longer be able to pervert and hunt us. Only God's Goodness and Mercy will be able to follow us all the days of our Lives (Ps 23:06).

This spirit not only comes to WAR:

This spirit comes to bring other hostilities; such as quarrels, disagreements in relationships. I saw this spirit as a big woman, defining herself as of a considerable size, number, quantity, magnitude or extent. It's great force, strong and having or exercising considerable authority, control or influence.

Hostility defines itself as unfavorable in health or well being. This spirit has the authority to affect our State of well being to inhibit us from being Healthy, Happy and Prosperous it also comes to bring disunity.

The Jezebel spirit truly comes to take your Peace. PEACE—the absence of war or other Hostilities, Freedom from quarrels, disagreements and to have harmonious relationships.

Harmony-being in agreement or harmony (being in one accord in feelings and action)

(St John 14:27) Christ said I give you Peace, not as the world giveth, give I unto you. Let not your Heart be troubled, neither let it be afraid. Christ gives us the Peace and Harmony not only in Warfare, quarrels and disagreements but also to be with one accord in our own feelings and actions.

CHAPTER TWO

THE DECEPTION FROM AUTHORITY

As stated in Chapter 1, GOD dealt with me in dreams to warn me about various attacks of warfare I was going to experience. In this Particular Dream, I saw two snakes in the top of my overseer's ceiling and a whole lot of black bugs on the walls all the way down to the baseboards. In the dream I was looking up at the two snakes being afraid and at all the bugs trying to get past them. I was afraid one of the bugs would get on me but I was able to get out without them getting on me.

When I awaken I was so afraid because it seems so real, I thought it was on my ceiling and walls what I had seen in the dream.

Two months later, it was my Pastor's Anniversary and the Prophet from my overseer's Church told my Overseer what GOD had revealed unto him while he was preaching.

GOD had revealed to him that it must be a changing of the Guards in order for GOD to bless the Ministry; That GOD needed a man in charge of the ministry now in order for it to continue to grow.

My overseer later called me and communicated to me what the Prophet had shared with him and what he believes the LORD was saying to him pertaining to the Ministry.

This is the man that three years earlier said he believes in Women in Ministry, That GOD calls Women to Pastor, Preach and Teach! This man Ordained Me as the Pastor for the Work.

After three years of Serving in the office of Pastor he wants me to step down and become the Mother of the Church, He wants to put a Man in Position.

I told him I don't believe GOD would birth the ministry through me and then after 3 years would change his mind and I was not in any blatant sin.

He said GOD just raised the ministry up through me just because I was the Mature one at that time and to get us away from our former pastor!

He said GOD never intended for a woman to lead in that capacity anyway, Also if I didn't agree nothing would go right for me and I would no longer be Anointed.

People would leave the Ministry, My daughter and her husband would turn against me, He spoke death over my Life and the Ministry, after that I had series of troubles.

One of my members died suddenly and my son who was fourteen at the time got into trouble, I had to move into an apartment within four days because of the trouble my son had gotten into. Most of the people left the ministry and it was like all of a sudden they hated me.

THE SEED OF DECEPTION HAS TAKEN ROOT

I believe that all these things were now happening because of my disobedience; by not stepping down as a Pastor. I am reminded of the Passage of Scripture in 1Kings 13:7-26 The sin of the Prophet, The LORD had given him instructions saying do not eat bread nor drink water nor return the same way again by the same way that he came to Bethel. But he allowed the Old Prophet to deceive him 1 kings 13:18, He said unto him I am also a Prophet as thou art, and an Angel spoke to me by the Word of saying; Bring him back with thee unto thine house, that we may eat bread and drink water. But he lied unto him!

So the Prophet went back with him and did eat bread and drank water.

Judgment came onto the Prophet for disobeying GOD and obeying the old Prophet.

It is very important that we follow the instructions of GOD! We must Respect and Submit to Leadership. But when we know that GOD has instructed us to do something we can not deviate from it. It cost this Prophet his Life!

The old prophet used his authority to deceive the young prophet. We must be aware of this weapon the enemy can use against us. My overseer tried to use this weapon against me: He said I am your overseer, don't you think GOD would show or let me know what's best for your ministry? This is a prime example of Spiritual Wickedness in High Places (Eph 6:12).

Again I cannot emphasize this enough: When GOD has spoken to us, We cannot allow anyone to cause us to deviate from it!

I am not trying to teach people not to Obey and Respect Authority, Only when it does not line up with what GOD has already said to you. This is the same thing the serpent did to Eve (Gen 3:1). Did GOD really say; You must not eat from the trees in the garden (vs. 3)? The woman said to the serpent' we may eat from the trees in the garden but not from the tree in the middle of the garden.

First thing, we must realize Satan always twists and perverts the Truth, He knew GOD did not say they could not eat from any of the trees. He will pervert and twist the truth to try to get you to compromise and agree to submit to his suggestions and his will. Ultimately to make you lose your dominion and authority where GOD has placed you (Gen 3:24).

Adam and Eve were banished from the garden, a place where GOD intended for them to cultivate and have dominion and authority over all creation. A place of Paradise!

Serpents symbolize the spirit of deception. In the case of the young prophet the old prophet uses his status as a Prophet to convince him to believe him. He also lied and told him an Angel spoke to him. The word of the LORD came directly to the Prophet!

Why would you receive a word from someone who is less than GOD over GOD himself as Truth? (Acts 5:29) Peter and the other Apostles said 'We ought to obey GOD rather than Man'.

When the spirit of deception comes never yield to it, instead give it the word and instructions GOD has already given unto you, just as Christ did in the wilderness.

Satan came to tempt him and each time he gave him the word (MT 4:4-10).

Temptations come to try to make you do wrong. Tests come to evaluate the determining presence quality or truth of something.

A test can also be a series of questions, problems or physical responses designed to determine your knowledge, intelligence and ability. A test purpose is ultimately used to cause or promote positive changes.

GOD never tempts us! He tests us.

Satan is the one who tempts in hope we would do or make the wrong choices (James 1: 13-14). No man can say he is tempted of GOD, for GOD cannot be tempted with evil neither tempted he any man.

The only way we can be tempted when we are drawn away of our own lust or desires and enticed or deceived. Once deception has conceived it brings forth sin and sin when it is finished, brings forth death.

Again we see even this spirit upon consummation is to kill. The spirit of deception from authority always works or stem from a lie. Satan did this to Eve. Old Prophet exemplifies (St John 8:44) Satan is a Liar and the father of Lies. (St John 8:47) He who is of GOD hears GOD'S Words.

Do not allow the thief to kill you, Obey what GOD has spoken unto you today!

CHAPTER THREE

THE FIERY DARTS

Once again the warning was given to me in a dream. I kept dreaming repeatedly about this white man with this long coat on and his long dark weapon was trying to kill me.

Every time I dreamed it, he would point the big dark weapon at me and say you are going to die. I became very afraid and thought I was going to die physically. I began having anxiety attacks. Some nights I was so afraid to go to sleep. I would prop all of my pillows high on the bed and I would say I am not going to sleep at all. I would have anxiety only at night, I couldn't feel my feet and my heart was beating extremely fast and I was having cold sweat, I began to have health problems.

I would be dizzy and lightheaded at night, Later I was diagnosed with High Blood Pressure. I was walking and looking in the flesh, I was not realizing my Warfare was not according to flesh (11 Cor. 10:3-5). (For the weapons of our warfare are not carnal, but mighty through GOD to the pulling down of strongholds) We are to use the weapons empowered by GOD to demolish anything that opposes God's will.

Cast down the warfare in our mind, I was told in a dream that the fire was coming (1 Pet. 4:12) We are not to think it strange concerning the fiery trial which is to try you, as though some strange thing happened unto you. 1 Peter 4:13 tells us to *rejoice*, inasmuch we are partakers of Christ's suffering it will also be a glory that will be revealed that we shall be glad also with exceeding joy. The key here is to rejoice when the fire comes.

Another *key or weapon* we can use in a fiery trial is not to bow down and worship anything other than God. In Dan. 3:14-18 Our faith and trust must be in our God.

We must acknowledge this fact that our trust is in God and that he is able to deliver us from the fiery furnace as the Hebrew boys did in Dan. 3:17.

During this time of attack, you will feel like you are a reproach, it's a time of great persecution. It appears that favor is not prevalent in your life, feel like you are alone. This is the way Christ felt in John 16:32 his hour had come for him to die, Disciples would be scattered and shall leave him alone, Yet he was not alone because the Father is with him. This is what we must realize, the father is still with us, even when no one wants to embrace you or fellowship with you or even when you are befriended, even in times whatever you try to do is of no avail and you are not received by many.

Christ told us they will not receive you because they did not receive him. He came unto his own and they received him not (John 1:11). You will be ostracized by family members, Peoples of God and the World (John 15:18,19). Then we go to the body of Christ and they want receive you. You must truly do what Christ told the disciples to do (MT 10:14). During this time you will truly feel like God is not with you.

God would always bring the Scripture in John 12:24—Except a corn of wheat fall in the ground and die, it abideth alone, but if it dies, it bringeth forth much fruit. This will bring great consolation.

The fire is never meant to destroy us, but to purify and purge us that we will be able to offer unto the Lord an offering in righteousness (Mal 3:23). Make sure we have our armour on upon going in the fire, the whole armour of God is what's going to keep us.

Notice when the Hebrews boys went in the fire they had on their armour Dan.3:21.

These men had on their coats, hosen, hats and other garments when they were cast in the fiery furnace.

The Princes, Governors, Captains and the Kings Counselors being gather together saw these men upon whose bodies the fire had no Power, the hair on their head was not singed, neither were their coats changed or destroyed. They did not even smell like they had been in a fire.

Our ARMOUR is seen also in Eph 6:14-18, we must wear Truth, have our heart full of Righteousness, have our feet should always be prepared to go to preach the Gospel of Peace, making sure we take utilize, operate in Faith because this is the way we will be able to quench or put out all the fiery darts of the wicked. Keep your Helmet of the Salvation on. That means to stay saved and also keep in mind that God will always Save, Rescue & Deliver us out of all Troubles and Afflictions.

Keep your sword of the Spirit which is the Word of God and always be ready to speak the Word in season Is. 50:4. Most theologians do not equate Eph 6:18 as part of the ARMOUR. I feel like Prayer must be included, Scriptures like Luke 18:1 That men ought to always Pray. We are to Pray always with all Prayer and Supplication in the Spirit and Watching with all perseverance for all saints. We are to pray humbly or earnestly in the Spirit and watch to wait with expectancy or in anticipation, with persistence, staying on course, standing strong in your faith and remembering your purpose in effort to support Prayer as part of the ARMOUR (Num 11:2). When Moses prayed unto the Lord, the fire was quenched. There are many references we could use to support Prayer, like the Hebrew boys and us, when we wear our ARMOUR the fire will have no Power over us.

CHAPTER FOUR

CHASED INTO
THE WILDERNESS

———◆◈◆———

After the fiery darts were launched at me I was chased into
the wilderness. I dreamed this same man with the long dark
weapon chased me through this long dark wilderness. After
running through the wilderness when I came out there was
this one house I saw and with a group of people standing
on the porch. I ran up on the porch and I knew they were
going to help me. The man had his weapon under his arm
and he passed me by and got in his car. In the dream I
thought I knew he should have seen me, but he went on.
The wilderness is an unsettled, uncultivated place. It is also
a bewildering perilous place. It can be a place of danger,
chance of injury and you can be exposed to the risk of harm
or loss, state of confusion, disorientation, confused about
your own identity, a place where numerous conflicts occur.

The enemy will make you think you are entangled and shut
in Ex. 14:3. This is what Pharoah said to the children of
Israel (They are entangled in the land and the wilderness

has shut them in). The enemy will try to make you think there is no way out. This is one of the weapons that the enemy will use against us. Once again the enemy will use fear as another weapon (Ex. 14:10) and the threat of death (Ex 14:11, 12).

During the time of my wilderness experience, I can attest to the fact that I suffered a tremendous loss. Everything I owned, I lost. I was in a state of confusion, seem like mostly everyone in the ministry had become confused and despondent.

I experienced conflict after conflict, at one point I doubted my call, I questioned my identity. I felt like the Israelites (Ex 14:12) they told Moses, "Let us alone, that we may serve the Egyptians" for it would have been better for us to serve the Egyptians than to die in the wilderness.

That's the way the enemy wants us to think, Egypt is a type of the world. He wants us to think being in the world is better than living for God. When we are in the wilderness, God will supernaturally bless us.

God wants us to do the following: (These are the keys found in Ex. 14:13-15.)

1. Fear not
2. Stand still or remain in peace
3. See his Salvation or Deliverance
4. Know that the Lord will fight for you
5. Keep going forward

We must realize the Lord is a man of war Ex. 15:3

He will dash in pieces the enemy Ex. 15:6

When you continue in the wilderness experience, God will preserve you from whatever the wilderness presents.

With the Israelites journey, God preserved them or maintained them in safety from injury, harm and peril. He will protect, provide and prepare things for you. Keep and maintain you as seen in Ex. 15:22-27

1. They were preserved from thirst
2. Preserved from hunger Ex. 16:12-35
3. Preserved from thirst again Ex. 17:1-7
4. Preserved from defeat Ex. 17:8-14
5. Preserved from chaos Ex. 18:1-11

NOTE: When we go through the wilderness Satan makes us want to murmur and complain. This is one of the most dangerous things we could do Num 14:22-30.

They did not hearken unto the voice of the Lord, they instead murmured against God and because they tempted him they did not enter into the Promise Land.

We want to make sure we are not guilty of the same sin and forfeit our Promises from God. Let us not follow after these examples but instead follow after the examples of Christ, in his temptations in his wilderness experience Mt 4:4-10

1. Live by every word that proceeded out of the mouth of God
2. (Verse 7) Make sure we don't tempt God
3. (Verse 10) Worship the Lord thy God and serve him only

These are the Keys or Weapons to use to be Victorious; Then Satan will leave (Mt 4:11)

Then Host of help will come—Heavenly Angels (Mt 4:12)

CHAPTER FIVE

DEMONS IN ANIMAL FORM

———◆—◆×◆—◆———

The attacks I experienced from demons were in animal form:

The animals Satan uses are:

- Snakes (Gen.3:1, Deut. 8:15, Deut. 32:24)
- Dogs (Ps. 22:16-20, II Pet. 2:22, Rev. 22:15)
- Pigs (Mt. 7:6)
- Scorpions (Luke 10:19)
- Dragons (Is. 43:19-20, Rev. 12:3-9)
- Locusts (Joel 1:4)

My first dream about snakes was when I saw the two snakes in the top of my overseer's ceiling in his church. I referred to it in the chapters previously. I saw all the black bugs on the walls coming all the way down to the baseboard. Now I realized these were scorpions. GOD had allowed me to know the characteristics of these spirits. They are people who are demon possessed and operate with the character or nature of demons n their different forms. I saw three snakes in my church in a vision. One was large and two were small. The snakes are treacherous people who always betray you. They betray your confidence and trust. They are not to be relied on. They are marked by deception. They always try to mislead you. I woke up one morning and the Spirit of the Lord spoke, that this is an anaconda. He was allowing me to know the types of serpents I was fighting. The administration of the anaconda is to suffocate you. To bring death, just as in the natural this serpent cuts your access to air, oxygen to cause death. This is how this spirit operates in the spiritual realm. It cuts off the supply, suppresses, stifles and causes tremendous lack, especially materially and spiritually. It also stops you from flowing in the spirit and will stifle and kill your anointing.

The dogs were demonic attacks I experienced also. I dreamed on several occasions this one sister in the church, her dog was chasing me. On one occasion in the dream, I out ran the dog and got in my apartment just in time. The next time I dreamed it her dog was chasing me but this time he bit my right hand and when I woke up I could still feel the pain in my hand. Dogs represent contemptible wicked person, a malicious despicable person. Contemptible people have open disrespect or willful disobedience. They love to disrespect and dishonor. The scripture in Ps. 22:16 states for the dogs have compassed or surrounded me. The assembly of the wicked has enclosed me about. They pierced my hands and my feet. Now I understand why this particular individual could come to church high on drugs with no regards. Never tried to hide her sinful lifestyle because this was the administration of this spirit in operation to show contempt and open disregard for the church and me.

Because I use to wonder how she could conduct herself like that, I use to say I would be embarrassed to conduct myself in that manner, because she was a member for about 4 years. It would perplex me. It made me wonder and ask GOD why no transformation or deliverance had taken place in her life. She did not want it. This was the manifestation of the spirit of the dog.

The pig was an attack I also experienced. This was not a dream. I was in my bedroom, I had just woken up and I saw a pig come in my room touch my right leg and go out of my bedroom window. It was the most eerie, horrible feeling I ever experienced. When it touched my leg, it was cold as ice and left a pain in my leg for days.

Pigs represent greedy, gross people. People that hold racist or sexiest views. These people always try to oppose you because of your gender and your race and will try to make you think in your mind, this is why GOD cannot use you to a certain capacity. They are unfriendly, uncompassionate people. Non affectionate people and will try to make you think you are weak because you show emotions and affection. That's why Christ said in Mt. 7:6 do not cast your pearls before swine, lest they trample them under their feet, and turn again and rend you. These are the characteristics of these people operating in the spirit of the swine or pig. We must be cognizance of giving our "pearls" unto them, because a pearl "defines" itself as *something that is prized for beauty or value*. They will have no respect for the beauty or value of the Holy things of GOD or you. They will beat them and you down, with the intent to bruise, crush, or destroy. They will treat you harshly and ruthlessly and inflict injury upon you again and again to keep you in a state of distress.

The scorpions that I saw in the dream they represent people who are malicious and spiteful. They have ill will towards you. Their purpose is to *torment*, hurt and humiliate you. They will do anything to vex, annoy and harass you. The word *torment* means:

To annoy, pester, harass or vex

A source of harassment, annoyance or pain

In *Rev. 9:3-5* the Locust that was released on earth was to torment man for not having the seal of GOD and was liken to the power as the scorpions already have on earth. *Vs. 5* states they were not to kill man but that they should torment them and that their torment was as the torment of a scorpion when he stings a man. So we see the spirit of the scorpion is sent to only torment us not to kill us. Sometimes we will wish death would come. In *Vs.6* those days, men will seek death and shall not find it, shall desire it and death will flee from them. Our consolation is what Christ said, "I give unto you *"power or authority"* to tread on *serpents* and *scorpions* and over *all* the *power* of the enemy and nothing shall by any means hurt you.

The dragon is what I saw in the dream that detached itself from its tail and went walking through my house. When I look at *Rev. 12:3*, the red dragon had 7 heads and 10 horns and 7 crowns upon his head. His tail drew the 3rd part of the stars of heaven and cast them to the earth and the dragon stood before the woman to devour her child as soon as it was born. I truly feel like I experienced this. This spirit was so fierce and intractable it truly tried to devour my children. The warfare with mu children intensified. Especially, with my youngest child, Satan really wanted to devour him. But the host of heaven fought for me and my children. In *Rev. 12:13,* just as the dragon *persecuted* the woman which brought forth the man child *vs.14* the woman was given to wings of a great eagle that she may fly into the wilderness into her place, where she is nourished for a time from the face of the serpent. I truly feel like that is what GOD did for me. Everything that the dragon casts out of his mouth is like a flood of water after me that I might be carried away or overtaken by my troubles. Just as in Rev. 12:16 the earth helped the woman and the earth opened her mouth and swallowed the flood which the dragon cast out of his mouth. The earth here represents the Spirit of GOD. Remember, Is. 59:19 states when enemy come in like a flood, the Spirit of the Lord shall lift up a standard against him. The Lord will lift up or raise up a banner or sign to indicate the rallying point in battle. The victory is yours always. Look for the sign as the indicator. The dragon comes to persecute you and try to devour your children but remember the Spirit of GOD and the Host of Heaven is there to fight for you. The dragon will not prevail.

Everything that came to bring death must pass by. Great analogy (Ex. 12:23) when the blood was applied upon door post and two side post the death angel or destroyer must pass over the door. It cannot come into your house to smite you.

The wilderness for the Israelites initially was the way GOD had chosen for them, first of all it was only supposed to be a three day journey. The purpose of the wilderness was so they could sacrifice unto the Lord or in other words pay homage and respect to the Lord (Ex. 3:18), (Ex. 3:17-18). It was the best and peaceful or safest way. GOD did not want to lead them through the way of the land of the Philistines even though it was the nearest because he didn't want them to change their minds and want to go back to Egypt if they experienced warfare with the Philistines. But because of their accusations, rebellion, murmuring and complaining they ended up wondering around and the older generation dying in the wilderness. GOD wants us to come through and go into the Promised Land. What has GOD promised you? Use the keys and weapons of GOD given here and come out victorious.

Locusts—to devour

Locust comes in swarms to devour or eat up. Their administration is to devour, destroy whatever remains. They come or travel in groups they never travel alone. When you see people that travel in groups from church to church their mission is to tear down a ministry. They always have a leader who has a Jezebel spirit presenting oneself to be very helpful, kind and knowledgeable. But their purpose and motives are completely opposite of what they portray.

CHAPTER SIX

THEY CAME TO DESTROY ME

They came to destroy me. This was very hurtful and surprising one Sunday. We were having a high time in the Lord. The Spirit of GOD was moving in a mighty way. One of the members began to vomit and fell down on the floor. We took the individual in the back of the church because we didn't want the children to see what was going on and how graphic it had become. Three other ministers along with me were working with the individual. We were praying and pleading the blood. All of a sudden the person started talking differently. One of the ministers said, what are you saying? Then the person did not respond. The minister asked the person who are you? The individual began to tell us their name. The minister asked why are you here? The individual responded I am here for the woman. The minister asked what woman? The individual replied again for the woman of this house. The minister asked, what do you want with the woman? The individual replied, to destroy the woman. The minister asked what have you done? The individual no longer responded. The thief was able to use this individual just as Judas was able to betray Christ. Because of dark areas of a person's heart, the enemy can use them as a vessel. Judas did it because of greed. (John 13:21) Christ testified that one would betray him. (John 13:27) Satan entered into Judas. Christ rebuked Peter because he wasn't mindful of the things of GOD, but things that be of man (Mark 8:33). He called him Satan and told him get thee behind me. I will probably never know how or in which way Satan used this individual to try to destroy me unless GOD reveals it. I was very afraid and intimidated once again. But in Matthew 10:26 Christ said fear not, for there is nothing covered, that shall not be revealed; and hid, that shall not be known. (Verse 27) Christ said what I tell you in darkness or in the night, speak in the light, what ye hear in the ear, preach upon the housetops. (Verse 28) Don't be afraid of them which can kill your body, but they are not able to kill your soul, but fear him which is able to destroy both soul and body in hell. This scripture was of great consolation to me. I began to think about the access the person had to me. Wondering what they had done or tried to do to me. GOD simply reminded me that I didn't have to be afraid. Just preach what I tell you to. Because I am the only one that can utterly destroy you. Respect me and do what I have called you to do. In (Rev. 9:11, 12) Apollyon, in Greek tongue, means the destroyer. Abaddon, in Hebrew tongue, means destruction they were demonic forces loosed from the bottomless pit. (Verse 1) A star fell from heaven. A fallen star is symbolic of Satan who was the king over them. The spirit of destruction has been released by Satan who is the destroyer. This was Satan's purpose (John 10:10) Thief came to steal, kill and destroy. Christ came that we might have life. (John 10:28) We need to confess this, Christ said I shall give unto us eternal life and we shall never perish, neither shall any man be able to pluck us out of His hand (Verse 29) My Father, which gave them me, is greater than all and no man is able to pluck or snatch us out of the Father's hand. This will combat the fear that arises if we truly believe and confess this. Let's not forget the purpose that the Son of GOD was manifested that He might destroy the works of the devil (1 John 3:7).

This spirit came to bring me into a state of spiritual destitution and material destitution. Destitution is extreme want of resources or the means of substance, complete poverty. That is the state that I had finely succumbed to. I was working on a secular job. We were down to four members. I lost everything I owned. Car and I was homeless for two months and can truly attest to no zeal and had almost lost all hope and faith in the Word of GOD.

CHAPTER SEVEN

THE DARK MAN ENTERS THE CHURCH

————◆◆◆————

The characteristics of the dark man are *mysterious,* exhibiting *evil characteristics,* sinister. The evil characteristics defines, itself as morally bad or wrong, wicked, causing ruin, injury or pain. It is harmful marked by anger, spite, maliciousness or destruction. It is an evil force or power that is personified causing much suffering, injury and destruction. This spirit always brings disaster and a series of inauspicious circumstances. This is the spirit of Satan himself that has to have an embodiment. So it operates strictly through personification. The dark man works to bring misfortune in such a way to try to force collapse and devastation. He will push so hard to cause widespread destruction, distress and total failure. This is his ultimate goal.

Upon this warfare, I dreamed a dark man came in the church. He had on all black clothing, even black sunshades. He was pure black. I saw him when he came through the door. He walked down the middle of the aisle of the church. He came directly in the pulpit where I was preaching. He came up and tried to push me off the pulpit and said, "I AM NOT FINISHED YET" and I woke up. After this seems like things got even worse for the church. People continued to leave or wouldn't even have visitors to come at this point. The finances of the church depreciated. Everything was under attack, even the praise and worship. This principality that I had now encountered was the ruler of darkness of this world. Christ told his disciples (John 14:30) the prince of this world cometh and hath nothing in me. This principality came to make things as dark and difficult for me as possible. (Dan. 10:13) The Heavenly messenger told Daniel the prince of the kingdom of Persia withstood him twenty one days. This principality came to hinder, stand against, oppose, hold up GOD's purposes and will for your life. The prince of Persia was an evil angel or demon who lures or abodes in the heavenly realm tried to keep the Israelites from returning home. We must understand principalities can control and exercise power over countries, cities, regions, nations and churches. This principality came to prevent the church from fulfilling its mandate. This prince has other lower ranking demons that are assigned to withstand you (Dan. 10:20). We have to understand we also have someone who will fight for us (Dan. 10:13) Michael, one of the chief princes. Please don't forget who our chief prince is "JESUS" (Is. 9:6) Wonderful, Counselor, the Mighty GOD, the Everlasting Father, "The Prince of Peace". That's why Michael was referred to as one of the chief princes because Christ is the Chief Prince that will always fight for us and help us. He is our present help in the time of trouble (Ps. 46:1) The sole purpose of this warfare with the ruler of darkness is to prevent the vision from coming to past. The angel of GOD was coming to give Daniel understanding about what was going to befall the people in latter days because the vision was for many days (Dan. 10:14). Daniel was only the vessel the Lord used to communicate the vision. The vision belongs to GOD. (Habakkuk 2:3) The vision is for an appointed time but at the end it shall speak and not lie, though it tarry, wait for it, it will surely come it will not tarry. Our assurance is, knowing that it will come to past. Just hold fast to the vision. Even when you become weary or weak GOD will come and strengthen you (Dan. 10:18). He will give you peace (Dan. 10:19). Because the spirit is a ruling spirit, as I mentioned earlier it has an administration of lower ranking demons also. It will seek out weak people whose hearts are not sold out unto the Lord. Remember in chapter 2 I talked about all the black bugs I saw on the wall of my overseer's church. These are the lower ranking demons that were loosed against me. Just as Christ has people he uses for his glory so does Satan have his servants (II Cor. 11:14-15). GOD showed in a dream this woman that was a member, she had on a red dress over top of me, holding me down as I began to pray she disintegrated and I was able to get up. I later found out she was practicing witchcraft against the ministry. I literally caught three people in the bathroom of the church with the lights off. Three ladies chanting things I had never heard. I stood outside the bathroom door and listened to them. We began to find other strange things. Someone had placed an upside down horseshoe by the front door of the church. I didn't know what it meant. One of the members told me, it is supposed to mean that your luck has run out. He removed it from in the front door for one (Eph. 5:11-12). We are instructed to have no fellowship with the unfruitful works of darkness but to expose them. We must understand their works are unfruitful (Gen. 5:19-22). Witchcraft is one of the works of the flesh that will manifest (Verse 20). I don't know why it was so hard for me to receive that. (Eph. 5:9) The Fruit of the Spirit is in all goodness, righteousness and truth. So we must understand the powers of darkness operate in the opposite ungodliness, unrighteousness, falsehood or deceit (verse 12). It is a shame to speak of the things that are done of them in secret. I later dreamed a voodoo doll was in the church bank bag. I saw it so clearly it had a straight pin in the heart of the voodoo doll with a white head on the pin. Also it had one regular straight pin in the right leg of the doll, this really frighten me. I was perplexed at this time. I kept saying GOD this can't be true. Is it real? Would someone go to this extent to come against the ministry? Why? The voodoo doll in the church bank bag: ***The pins symbolize immobility***.

> *Pin*—immobilize, to impede movement or use
> *Immobile*—stop from moving
> *Heart*—the vital center and source of one's being
> *Leg*—(Hebrew)—fig. of man's weakness
> *Leg*—(Webster)—supporting part
> *Source*—the point at which something springs into
>   being from which it derives or is obtained.

This weapon Satan used was to penetrate the people's hearts in such a way to prevent and inhibit them from giving and supporting the church. If a person's heart is not into something it will be difficult for them to do whatever is expected of them. So Satan used this weapon to stop them, because in their hearts they didn't have a desire to work or support. The pin I saw with the head on it in the dolls heart shows the control it had because the heart is the vital source of one's being. It deprived them from having the ability to go forward in being a blessing. The pin in the leg, symbolized them becoming weak and unable to support, truly unable to move forward in any capacity. But I truly saw and lived through the manifestations of the attacks. The offerings and tithes were so low, as only by the grace of GOD we survived. The people that were left had gotten in a state where they no longer wanted to be faithful in their giving. You see where that dark spirit entered it pushed me off the pulpit. He came to apply so much pressure against me for the purpose of trying to remove me. He really wanted me to quit. I lived by this world (2 Tim. 1:12) GOD is able to keep that which is committed unto him. (Verse 12) **For the which cause I also suffer these things: nevertheless I am not ashamed: for I know whom I have believed, and am persuaded that he is able to keep that which I have committed unto him against that day.**

That no weapon formed against me will not be able to prosper. Continue to disarm and displace the principalities and powers that have been loosed against me. I thank you that you said in your word, that your son, Jesus Christ, came as a light in the world and whosoever believes in him shall not live in darkness. You also said if I follow Him, I will not walk in darkness. They can no longer hinder me. I thank you for your light operating in my life all the days of my life. Amen! Remember, just in chapter 3 we must wear our armor also to stand against the ruler of darkness of this world, which is a principality and power also (Eph. 6:14-18).

CHAPTER EIGHT

THE SABOTEUR WAS CAUGHT

———◆◀◆▶◆———

Again in a dream, I dreamed my sister and I were going somewhere and we just happened to go to the church. We caught the man upstairs in the church. The man was there to sabotage the church and we caught him. The word sabotage defines itself with several definitions.

1. Destruction of property or obstruction of normal operations as by enemy agents in war
2. Treacherous actions to defeat or hinder a cause or endeavor
3. Deliberate subversion

In Exodus 22:4, if the thief be certainly found in his hand alive, whether to be ox or ass or sheep, he shall restore double. Once we can identify who the thief is and what?? He is stealing and he is discovered or come upon suddenly, unexpectedly, or accidently he must pay restitution. In Hebrew restitution is (Shalam) to be safe in mind, body or estate to be completed, make amends, give again, make good, repay, pay again, make to be at peace. Make prosperous, restore.

Everything this thief tried to do by sabotage will no longer be able to prevail against the church. All the weapons used to try to destroy, hinder and stop the normal operations of the church will not continue. The Word in exodus 22:4 said because he was caught he must give back. Everything that restitution defines must have transpired in the church now. (Phil. 1:6) we must be confident of this very thing, that he which hath begun a good work in you will complete it until the day of Jesus Christ. (Proverbs 16:7) when a man's ways please the Lord, he maketh even his enemies to be at peace with him.

In Joel 2:25 GOD said he will restore to you the years that the locust hath eaten and the cankerworm, the caterpillar and the palmerworm. Verse 26—and he shall eat in plenty now and be satisfied and praise the name of the Lord and we will never be ashamed.

Some things to expect in restitution and restoration are (Is. 54:13)

1. All thy children shall be taught of the Lord and great shall be their peace
2. In righteousness shall thou be established
3. Thou shalt be far from oppression
4. Thou shalt not fear
5. Shall not have terror
6. Whoever shall gather against you shall fall
7. No weapon formed against you shall prosper

8. Every tongue that rise up against you shall be condemned

A key factor to always remember is when a thief is caught he must always "pay restitution"

It is truly restoration time. A time of refreshing for the body of Christ (Acts 3:19). In Zech. 5:3 for everyone that steal shall be cut off. Everything that we have lost in warfare will be given back now. (Eccl. 1) To everything there is a season and a time to every purpose under heaven. Everything in life has its appointed time or cycle. Here in this warfare with the saboteur he worked against us in many different capacities. Just as in Eccl. 3:3, it's time to kill and time to heal. If the thief tried to kill, it's now timed to be healed. If he has torn down things now it's time that things will be built up. If all you have done in this season of warfare is weep. Now you can laugh. If you have been mourning it's time to dance. Been in war? A time for peace is now. (Ps. 30:5) weeping may endure for a night but joy cometh in the morning. The night season is over when the thief is caught. Joy will come because when your morning season comes, joy is one of the attributes of morning. This is the time of great victory.

CHAPTER NINE

SHE DIED
IN THE CHURCH

Again in a dream, my daughter and I were having a conversation. I was saying in the dream, it sure is a lot of peace in here. My daughter agreed, but she said you must bind the spirit up because you know she was being poisonous because if you don't bind that spirit up she will haunt you.

GOD was allowing me to see in this dream that the spirit was going to cease from victory over the church. I identified this spirit again as the Jezebel spirit that had been in operation against the ministry and me. As I talked in Chapter 1, now she had come to injure, harm and bring death. Now the season had come that GOD wanted me to walk in power and authority. I have the authority to bind the spirit, not allow the spirit access to operate in the church. This principality will no longer pursue or follow me (Mt. 16:19). It is truly time for the absence of war in this magnitude and other hostiles, freedom from strife, quarrels, disagreements, inner contentment time to have harmonious relationships.

(Eccl. 3:2) It's a time to be born, time to die. Look at this concept, if it's a time to be born and a time to die, if this Jezebel spirit has died in the church, then it is time for **the Elijah spirit to be birthed** in the church now. (Mal. 4:5-6) GOD said, "I will send you Elijah the prophet before the coming of the dreadful day of the Lord." Verse 6—He shall turn the heart of fathers to the children and the heart of the children to the fathers. Everything the Jezebel spirit has done to bring division, destitution and death is going to turn around. When it is peace time expect things to change for the good. GOD is going to reverse every cause. **Restoration (Mt. 17:11) Christ told disciples Elijah would come and restore all things.** "EXPECT A CHANGE, DON'T MISS THE SHIFT."

CHAPTER TEN

THE ATTACK THROUGH MY CHILDREN

———◆◆◆———

In this dream I was moving all of my belongings, was in this very large tractor trailer. The truck was so big and it didn't have an end to it. This man was trying to stop me from moving, because he couldn't stop me, he sent two teenagers to my house to deceive me and tried to stop me. Within a couple months after this dream, I began to see the manifestation of the dream. It stated first with my youngest son, who was 16 at this time. He became very rebellious and disobedient. He began to disobey and defy me and all authority. A lawless spirit began operating in him. He began to break the law, going to jail, fighting me, destroying my property and embarrassing me in any capacity. My oldest son began to act like he hated me also. They both would fight me and treated me very unkind. The warfare with my youngest son was the worst. He verbally abused me everyday. The enemy used him to attack me in many ways. Because of his encounters with the law, I was tormented. Satan used the fear I had of him going to jail against me. My boys would say things to me like, why don't you kill yourself? No one likes you anyway. When my youngest son was on house arrest for 2 ½ months I was tormented. I had to put locks on all the windows, change the deadbolts to keyed deadbolts in effort to keep him from leaving the house. He would have episodes of rage so strongly that he would kick holes in the walls. One night he took a hammer and broke out windows then he called the police and told them I was crazy. He asked them to take him back to detention because I had locks on everything. They told him it was within my right to have locks on the windows and that I had not broken any laws by doing this. I believed this attack was more severe and devastating to me than any of the prior attacks. I was overwhelmed by this attack. I had hardly any physical strength left. I felt like it had been zapped. I was so distracted by this warfare. I didn't have any peace. When I would go to church, I would have to have someone at my house to stay with my son to make sure he wouldn't leave. If you leave your house when you are on house arrest without a scheduled window, you will automatically be certified to state reformatory school. This was my biggest fear. I was afraid to go anywhere. I didn't want to leave my house in fear of him leaving also. I didn't go anywhere at this time, except to church. I didn't have any peace while I was at church. I would call every few minutes to check on him. This was a time of great distraction for me. It seemed as though the enemy was winning. I was definitely not moving. I was stagnated. I was almost dead. My blood pressure had elevated so that my doctor had to put me on two medications. The weapons of discouragement, fear and deceit the enemy was using was prevailing. (Neh. 4:8) The enemies conspired all of them together to come and fight against Jerusalem and to hinder it. This is what was happening to me. This is what

I should have done (Neh. 4:9) Pray unto GOD and set a watch against them day and night.

Discouragement is one of the greatest weapons that Satan can use against you, because discouragement steals your strength. The strength of the bearers of burdens is decayed and there is much rubbish; so that we are not able to build the wall. (Neh. 4:10) This will cause you not to be able to identify who is fighting you. The purpose is to kill you and cause the work to cease. (Neh. 4:11)

I was not using my weapons. I was not walking in faith and hope and I was not using my sword or none of my armour at this point. I can say this was the weakest point I had ever experienced. All I knew at this point was that I stilled loved God; I still lived a Holy Life. I use to tell GOD, you know I love you. Why am I going through all this? GOD said, It is not to destroy you, but to build you. (Jude 1:20) Build yourselves up in your most holy faith and pray in the Holy Spirit.

(Jude 1:21) Keep yourselves in GOD's love as you wait for the mercy of our Lord Jesus Christ to bring you eternal life.

CHAPTER ELEVEN

They Strenghten the Warfare

In a dream, I saw what appeared to be my mother run across the room to my youngest son's room and touched his mouth. I did not want her to touch him. I was trying to speak and rebuke her but I couldn't get the words out. It felt like something was holding me down because I wanted to get up and stop her but I couldn't. I saw my mother in this dream in the state she was in before she became ambulatory. My mother is deceased. She has been deceased for 10 years. Upon becoming ambulatory she could hardly walk, but in the dream she was running on her tip toes. This was very upsetting to me. When I was able to speak I started pleading the blood of Jesus. When I awaken I was so afraid because it seemed so real. Before I dreamed this, it seemed that my youngest son was doing better. The night that I dreamed this he was not at home. He came home the next day in a rage, cursing me, displaying the same out of control behavior. I was asking GOD to reveal to me what was going on. My son was doing things that could have caused him to lose his life. I would pray and ask GOD to have mercy on him. Save and deliver him. I kept asking GOD to give me the interpretation of this dream. Then GOD took me to (Dan. 10:16) Daniel said, one like the similitude of the sons of men touched my lips, then I opened my mouth and spake and said unto him that stood before me, O my Lord, by the vision my sorrows are turned upon me, and I have retained no strength. GOD let me know, what I had seen pertaining to what appeared as my mother touching my son's lips was what Daniel experienced. This demonic spirit came and reinforced and strengthened itself in my son. This spirit manifested itself like the similitude or likeness of my mother. No strength remained in my son to resist this demon. It was as if he was totally out of control, to the point that I had to separate myself from him because of the fear that I had of him.

I should have been praying (Eph. 3:16) That Christ would grant to me according to the riches of his glory and to be strengthen with might by His Spirit in the inner man. Daniel was touched by the heavenly angel, but my son was touched by a fallen angel, which is a demon. To fortify its strength within him, I began to confess (Ps. 18:1-3) I love thee Lord, my strength. The Lord is my rock, my fortress and my deliverer; my GOD, my strength, in whom I will trust; my buckler, and the horn of my salvation, and my high tower. I will call upon the Lord, who is worthy to be praised: so shall I be saved from mine enemies. This is what I prayed for my son repetitiously. I would especially say save and deliver my son from the enemy. I would intercede on his behalf.

Regardless of the intensity of the warfare, it is not greater than the power of GOD. GOD would always remind me of (Rom. 13:1)—Let every soul be subject unto the higher powers. For there is no power but of GOD and the powers that be are ordained of GOD. GOD will allow evil to rule for a time, but we must remember the greater lives in us. (I John 4:4) Greater is he that is in you, than he that is in the world. The greater one is GOD. Key weapon for us to use is to make sure we stay in the presence of GOD. (Ps. 16:11) In his presence is the fullness of joy. (Neh. 8:10) told the people the joy of the Lord is your strength.

Hebrew—Joy—(simchak) gladness, pleasure, exceedingly gladness

Hebrew—Strength—(maouz) a fortified place, a defense

When we allow the pleasure, gladness of the Lord to operate in our life we will be those people who walk in strength. You see the joy will operate as our defense. See how this becomes a key. We will be able to lock or unlock, do or undo whatever thinks it has fortified itself in our lives that Satan has sent. The joy becomes a defense mechanism. This is one of the ways we can protect ourselves against attacks of the enemy.

CHAPTER TWELVE

WE MUST STRENGTHEN OUR HANDS

In (Neh. 2:18) Nehemiah exhorted the people to build and strengthen their hands for this good work. I would like to admonish the body of Christ to strengthen your hands for the work of the Lord. In Nehemiah chapters 4, 5, 6, it gives explicit instructions on building, what to expect upon building. These chapters address the opposition and weapons that "the enemy" will use to try to hinder, prevent the work. Also we will see Nehemiah as a "type of God" preparing "arming a people for battle."

(Neh. 4:6) Have to have a mind to work

(Neh. 4:9) Have to pray and watch

(Neh. 13) Position people with their weapons

In (Neh. 4:16-23)—You will see the administration and strategy Nehemiah used for the warfare.

(vs. 14) Chapter 4 Nehemiah exhorts the people not to be afraid of their enemies, and to remember that GOD is the one who fights for us and gives us victory, to let the people know they must also be willing to fight for our brethren, sons, daughters, wives and your houses.

(vs. 16) shows or exemplify to us how important it is to work, utilize our weapons and support the work.

(vs. 19) they realized the work was great and large and also that they were separated upon the wall there was no unity or division.

(vs. 20) was a call to unity, Nehemiah eluded to the fact that when you hear the trumpet sound, come together, and our GOD shall fight for us. It is significant to be unified.

In (Ps. 133:1-3) David said, It was good and pleasant for brethren to dwell together in unity.

He likened it to the precious ointment upon the head that ran down the beard of Aaron. And as the dew of Herman that descended upon the mountains of Zion, where the Lord commanded the blessings, even life forever more.

Another example of the power of unity (Gen. 11:1-9)—The tower of Babel, the people had a mind to work together in unity to build a city and a tower whose top would reach heaven. The Lord came down to see the city and the tower, which the children built. And he said, the people are one and they have one language and they begin to do this and nothing will be able to restrain them from doing this. What they have imagined to do.

GOD conferred with the trinity, and said, Let us go down and confound their language so they will not be able to understand one another. And the Lord scattered them upon the face of the earth and they left off or stop building the city. We can see a twofold strategy here. GOD himself knew and allowed us to see the power of

1.   Having a mind to work.
2.   Being in unity and harmony.

These are two keys we see in operation here that will allow you to build successfully. The other two keys that GOD used here to bring the work to a halt or cease:

1.   Confusion
2.   Division or Depression

These are also great keys or weapons that Satan uses against us also.

Weapons Satan use against us in (Neh. 4:1-6) display the

1.   Opposition through ridicule
2.   Opposition through threat of attack (Neh. 4:7-9)
3.   Opposition through discouragement (Neh. 4:10-12)
4.   Opposition through extortion (Neh. 5:1-11)
5.   Opposition through compromise (Neh. 6:1-4)
6.   Opposition through slander (Neh. 6: 5-9)
7.   Opposition through treachery

Please look in depth at these 7 weapons carefully, especially the last one that Tobiah and Sandballat used against Nehemiah which was treachery. They had hired the false prophet to prophesy against him and (vs. 11-12) to promote fear in him and to sin to cause the work to cease because Nehemiah didn't receive the prophecy nor the spirit of fear he was able to complete the work. This is the same example we must follow after to complete the work that GOD was given unto our hands. We must not receive and yield to the attacks and weapons of the enemy. We must strengthen our hands for work, must be like Joshua, strong and courageous. Be strong and very courageous that we may wherever we go. (Joshua 1:7)

CHAPTER THIRTEEN

WE MUST USE THE KEYS

Again in a dream I went in this place. I saw two young men sitting in these seats handcuffed together. I went in and took the keys. It was two keys in a container sitting on what looked like a podium. One was a big gold key and the other one was silver. The big gold key was going to allow me to get on this airplane. I am reminded of the scripture in Rev. 1:18 where Christ said, I am he that liveth and was dead, and behold, I am alive for evermore, Amen: and have the keys of hell and death. We know that Christ was crucified died and arose, because when he said I liveth because I am the resurrection. He took the keys to death and judgment. I look at this also when he says he took the keys to death and hell also as Him saying he has authority over the kingdom of Satan because until that time Satan had authority over death and hell until Christ death, burial and resurrection. I believe this is why I saw the two keys but, it is not limited to two keys literally. It is showing me we have power over the kingdom of Satan also. It is time to use the keys!

Taking the Keys

We must take the keys to the Kingdom realizing Christ told Peter in Mt.16:19, I will give unto thee the keys to the Kingdom of Heaven and whatever you bind on earth shall be bound in heaven and whatsoever you loose on earth shall be loosed in heaven.

Take—1. To get into ones possession by "force or skill"
       2. To seize with "authority"

Force—A power made operative against resistance

We have the same authority. We must take those keys with authority or force. Peter had been given a right to enter into the Kingdom of Heaven. The word—bind in Greek defines itself as "to declare forbidden." In Greek the word—loose means to allow

In Mt.11:12 "The Kingdom of heaven suffers violence and the violent take it by force. The Kingdom of heaven suffers many violations but we must press with great intensity as enforcers with all might and power by the Holy Spirit. We must take these keys, possess or utilize these keys regardless of the resistance that will be encountered from Satan. This is how we take it by force.

The Keys We Must Use:

1. The Name of JESUS—(because everything is to bow or submit Phil. 2:10)
2. The Blood of JESUS—(keeps from death or destruction Ex. 12:22-23)

3. The Word of GOD—(heals and delivers, brings things into fruition Ps. 107:20 and Is. 55:11)
4. The Shield of Faith—(removes mountains Mt.17:20)
5. Prayer—(miracles, healing James 5:16-18)
6. Fasting—(favor, healing, deliverance Mt.17:21 and Esther 5:2)
7. Ask—(things to be given Mt. 7:7)
8. Seek—(find what you're looking for Mt. 7:7)
9. Knock—(doors opened Mt. 7:7)

When we use the *Name of Jesus* as a key we will see everything yield, submit, or surrender to the will or authority of Christ. They will give into the authority, power or desires of Christ. They will allow one to be subject to Christ.

In Ex. 12:22-23 we saw the application of the blood of the lamb which was a type and shadow of the *Blood of JESUS* preserved and protected them from death. When the blood was applied over the door post and side post which is symbolic to us as the blood of Christ being over us and on both sides of us which means they were simply covered by the blood. So when we are covered by the blood it will cause everything that comes to bring death to pass us by.

The *Word of GOD* is another key to use, we see examples here of healing and deliverance as a result of utilizing this key. GOD told them in "Ps. 107:20" he would send his word to heal and deliver them so we can expect restoration in the three-fold realm, Spiritually, Financially and Physically. Expect to be whole, sound and complete. In Isaiah 55:11 we see the analogy of GOD's word accomplishing what he sends it to do. We will see things come into fruition and manifestation.

The *Key of Faith* causes those things that seem huge and impossible to dissipate. They will be eliminated, taken away. We have so many examples in the Bible about faith we could use. I chose this scripture because it speaks more universally, because so many things can stand as a mountain in so many of our lives. Whatever that thing that seems huge and impossible unto you that stands as your mountain. I was intrigued because the scripture in "Mt. 17:20" states; if you have faith as a grain of a mustard seed we can say to this mountain be thou removed speaks to those who only have a small measure of faith. We can speak to this mountain, remove ye hence to yonder place and it shall remove, and nothing shall be impossible unto you! This is a powerful statement because a mustard seed is a very small seed. In Mt. 13:31: The parable of mustard seed describes the Kingdom of heaven to a grain of mustard seed vs. 32 says the mustard seed is the least of all seeds but when it is grown, it is the greatest among herbs and becomes a tree.

This should be great consolation to us. If we only have a small amount of faith at the present time and if we exercise the smallest amount of faith we have it and it will grow and become great. If we truly believe we will see that nothing is impossible unto us. It's ok to try your faith beginning in small things and allow your faith to grow, to the point that it will truly become that shield that will also combat the fiery darts of the enemy also.

The *Key of Prayer* is considered the master key. A master key is a key that unlocks different locks. One definition says a master key unlocks many locks. Another said it opens all other locks. So in my analogy when I look at prayer I see it as a key that will allow all of the other keys we have discussed to open and operate in our lives. Prayer has so many "facets and administrations". In John 15:7 Christ said, "If ye abide in me, and my words abide in you, you shall ask what ye will and it shall be done unto you". If we expound on this scripture Christ was communicating unto the disciples if you live, stay in me, give place to me, have a relationship with me, remain with me and my words live in you, stay with you, if you give place to my words, spend time in my words, build a relationship based upon my words, let my words remain in you and most of all live by my words, you can ask what you will and I will do it for you. I call this passage of scripture in John 15:7, THE MASTER KEY OF PRAYER BECAUSE IT ALLOWS US TO KNOW THAT WE CAN ASK WHATEVER WE WANT ACCORDING TO HIS WILL AND IT SHALL BE DONE, THIS WILL TRULY UNLOCK ALL THINGS.

James 5:16-17, another example of healing and miracles. We see the effectual fervent prayers of the righteous availeth much. Then we see the miracle with Elijah praying about the rain. First for it not to rain, then for rain and we see the manifestation of both prayers.

The *Key of Fasting*—We see the key of fasting opening doors by giving favor, healing and deliverance. In Esther 4:16

Esther called for all the Jews to fast for 3 days and nights for favor to go into the king's court. So that her people would not be destroyed and she indeed received favor and was promoted to Queen. In Mt. 17:21 by fasting the lunatic son was healed and delivered. Christ told his disciples that this kind goeth out but by prayer and fasting. Some things cannot be made whole and recovered except you pray and fast. We must pray and ask GOD about the things that fasting can unlock.

The *Key of Asking* in Mt. 7:7 states that if we ask it can be given. James 4:2 We have not because we ask not. Mt. 18:19 Christ said if two of you shall agree on earth as touching anything that they shall ask, it shall be done for them. Mt. 21:22 All things, whatsoever ye shall ask in prayer, believing, ye shall receive.

The *Key of Seeking* when you seek you shall find what you are seeking. Mt. 6:33 is the number one thing we should seek, which is the Kingdom of GOD. If we seek the Kingdom first and all its righteousness, all other things we need and desire will or shall be added unto us. I think it really pleases GOD when we seek Him, because he said in Heb. 11:6 he is a rewarder of them that diligently seek him. What do you think our rewards are? I believe his rewards are the desires of our hearts. The things we need and desire. Mt. 7:7 if we seek and search out things we will find, discover, uncover and receive those things.

The *Key of Knocking* tells us in Mt. 7:7 if we knock the doors will be opened, but this is predicated upon letting Christ in our house first. In Rev. 3:20 Christ said, BEHOLD, I STAND AT THE DOOR AND KNOCK, if any man, hear my voice and open the door, I will come into him, and will sup with him and him with me. Remember this text was written to the Laodicean church which was in an apostate condition. He rebuked them for being a lukewarm church. When he referred to the term "sup" with he was trying to appeal to them to truly allow him to be their Lord and Savior, to have genuine fellowship with him. When he said, he stands at the door and knock he was not talking about a literal door but he was referring to their hearts. If they could discern him as Lord and receive him, truly accept him in all their ways, take up their cross, deny themselves and follow him. Then they would have an intimate relationship and fellowship. If we never really open the door for Christ as Lord we could never have the doors open that we desire. Even if we did, in Mark 8:36 what would it profit a man to gain the whole world and lose his soul? "Saints use your Keys in JESUS name and walk in victory".

The only way we can strengthen our hands in summary is by utilizing everything GOD has revealed to us in this book. We must use all of our weapons, Keys and make sure we have on our whole armour, and in order to be able to stand against the wiles of the devil as in Eph. 6:11.

Greek—Strengthen—to set fast, to turn resolutely in a certain direction, to confirm, establish

In Zech 10:1 as ye of the Lord rain in the time of the latter rain, so the Lord shall make bright clouds and give them showers of rain to everyone's grass in the fields. Zech chapter 1 deals with the redemption of the Lords people. GOD is going to bless his people and cause brightness and a supernatural supply for his people. Verse 6 the Lord said, he will strengthen the house of Judah and will save the house of Joseph and will bring them again to place them, far. He has mercy upon them and they will be as though he had not cast them off. He is going to set them fast, establish them and confirm them.

Verse 8 of Zech 1 he is going to gather us, redeem us and increase us.

Verse 12 he is going to strengthen us in the Lord and we shall walk up and down in his name.

Luke 22:31-32 Christ told Peter, Satan hath desired to have you, that he may sift you as wheat, but I have prayed for you, that your faith fail not, and when thou art converted, strengthen thy brethren.

Verse 33 Peter told him he was ready to go with him both into prison and to death but Christ knew he was going to deny him. Peter had not yet encountered this trial yet. But Christ knew what he was going to do. That's why he told Peter when you are converted, strengthen your brethren.

Greek—Converted—come again, go again, turn again, to revert

Web—Converted—1. Persuade or induce to adopt to a particular religion, faith or belief
2. To change something into another form, substance, state, product, transform, to undergo conversion

Web—Revert—to return to a former condition, practice, subject or belief

Christ was saying when you come back again to your faith, belief, state of transformation to your former condition and believe after your denial of me and take a firm stand in your belief then you will be able to strengthen your brethren. You will be able to lead them in the right direction. Confirm and establish your brethren in the faith. Just like with Peter, Satan has desired to have us, but thank GOD Christ is still interceding on our behalf. I hope that after reading this book we are all converted in our mind and hearts and can truly strengthen someone else.

In Peter 5:6-10 we are told to humble ourselves under the mighty hand of GOD, that he may exalt us in due time.

Dorothy A. Weatherford

Casting all our care upon him, for he careth for you. Be sober, be vigilant because your adversary, the devil, as a roaring lion, walketh about, seeking whom he may devour. Whom resist steadfast in the faith, knowing that the same afflictions are accomplished or experienced by brethren that are in the world. But the GOD of all grace, who hath called us unto his eternal glory by Christ Jesus after that you have suffered a while, make you perfect, establish, strengthen and settle you. To him be Glory and Dominion forever and ever.

AMEN

CHAPTER FOURTEEN

MESSAGE TO SMYRNA

———◆◆◆———

To the churches that operate in the spirit of Smyrna. Christ knows our works, tribulations and poverty, but we are rich and he knows the blasphemy of them which say they are Jews and are not, *but* are the "*Synagogue of Satan*". Rev. 2:9

In *verse 10*: He tells us to fear none of those things which thou shall suffer, behold the devil shall cast *some of you* in *prison*, that you may be *tried*, and ye shall have tribulation *10 days*; be thou faithful unto death and he will give thee a crown of life.

The name Smyrna meant "*Myrrh*" which was used as a fragrance for the anointing of dead bodies (John 19:39). This church represents the persecuted church. When you look at the statement Christ made when he talked about their works, tribulations and poverty. Then he told them that they are rich. He was allowing them to know that they were rich in spiritual things and that the anointing would be heavy over their lives. They would have to endure and tolerate all those who pretend to be people of GOD but were not. But instead are sold out for Satan and are used mightily by Satan to intern us and hinder and try to keep us blocked from being free in GOD. They are false brethren. Paul talked about this in Galatians 2:4-6. Verse 4—because of false brethren unaware brought in, who came in privily to spy out our liberty which we have in Christ Jesus that they might bring us into bondage.

(Verse 5) To whom we gave place by subjection, no, not for an hour, that the truth of the gospel might continue with you.

(Verse 6) But of those who seemed to be somewhat, whatsoever they were, it maketh no matter to me: GOD accepteth no man's person, for they seemed to be somewhat in conference added *"nothing to me"*. GOD wants us to be aware of these *unbelievers* who will infiltrate true worshipper's churches. Their main purpose is to spy out and examine the *believer's liberty* or *freedom*. But we must always remember their ultimate aim is to bring the true Christians into bondage. Another key factor for us is to remember that they really are not spiritual assets to a ministry. Remember what Paul said in (vs.6) they *added nothing to him*. This is and always should be an indication to us as we examine the character and the operation of these people. We must understand that when we give them place, position and authority in our churches that they can hinder or interfere with the truth of the gospel from continuing. That's why Paul stated that he did not give them place not even for an hour.

Just like in the beginning of this book in (Chapter 1) I talked about the woman that came to fight me and I went to jail, we see Christ reminding us in (Rev. 2:10) that some of us will suffer greatly, be put in prison or heavy bondage, have great trials, tribulations but admonishing us to remain faithful unto GOD until death. He will give us a *crown of life*. We will have a *crown*.

Crown—an emblem, diadem

A crown is something worn or seen. He is going to make us that emblem. (Is. 62:1-4) GOD said, (verse 1) for Zion's sake I will not hold my peace and for Jerusalem's sake I will not rest until the righteousness thereof go forth as brightness, and the salvation thereof as a lamp that burneth.

(Verse 2) And the Gentiles shall see thy righteousness and all Kings thy *glory*, and thou shalt be called by a new name, which the mouth of the Lord shall name.

(Verse 3) Thou shalt also be a "*crown of glory*" in the hand of the Lord, and a royal diadem in the hand of thy GOD.

(Verse 4) Thou shalt no more be termed "*Forsaken*" neither shall thy land anymore be termed "*Desolate*", but shalt be called Hephzibah and thy land Beulah for the Lord *delighteth* in thee, and thy land shall be married.

Just like in the natural prisoners are guarded, Satan uses this type of administration to keep us confined. Satan usually uses people close to you or has access to you, like a best friend or family member. He will send people to guard and keep you interned. One will feel like they cannot escape his control. This is why we must Pray, Fast and use the keys mentioned earlier. Just as Christ reminded us—JUST BE

FAITHFUL UNTO GOD AND YOU WILL RECEIVE YOUR CROWN OF LIFE!

GOD is truly going to restore us in every aspect he will cause his righteousness and glory to rest upon us for everyone to see. He will do it suddenly. We will no longer appear to be forsaken, nor desolate. No more barrenness. We will be joined to the Father in truth and holiness like never before. We will see the manifestation of his glory.